Urn detail, West Portico

Edited by James B. Patrick

Designed by Donald G. Paulhus

Printed in Hong Kong

Published by
Fort Church Publishers, Inc.
Little Compton, RI 02837

Distributed by
Roosevelt-Vanderbilt Historical Association
P.O. Box 235
Hyde Park, NY 12538

VANDERBILT MANSION

Photography by Richard Cheek

Introduction by Charlotte Ofca Scholl

Published by Fort Church Publishers, Inc.
in cooperation with
Roosevelt-Vanderbilt Historical Association

The White Bridge

The Height of the Gilded Age

On a pleasant day in 1895, Frederick W. Vanderbilt was yachting up the Hudson River to the Ogden Mills estate at Staatsburg, New York, about ninety miles north of New York City. A few miles south of his destination, he was captivated by the sight of a magnificent plateau, dominated by splendid trees. This was Hyde Park. Vanderbilt, enchanted, at once learned that the property was for sale and happily purchased it from the estate of Walter Langdon, Jr., for $125,000. This price included a mansion, outbuildings, gardens and green-houses, a farm, and approximately 600 acres of land. Although the property was overgrown and neglected, Hyde Park in time was to become Frederick Vanderbilt's great pride. Here Vanderbilt, who held a degree in horticulture, would practice scientific farming, gardening, forestry, and conservation. The majestic setting of Hyde Park afforded him great contentment and satisfaction for the rest of his life.

The beauty of the river, readily accessible with the development of the rail-roads, and the availability of large tracts of land within easy traveling distance of New York City, drew wealthy families to the mid-Hudson valley. The Hudson River area around Hyde Park was described as "the Rhine of the United States."

When Frederick Vanderbilt bought Hyde Park, he entered an august com-pany. The Vanderbilts joined the Roosevelt, Morgan, Newbold, Rogers, Lewis, Norrie, Mills, Astor, Delano, and Livingston families who had established pala-tial estates on the east bank of the Hudson River referred to as *millionaires' row*. Some of these property owners were moneyed because of their recent achieve-ments in industry and commerce and strove to acquire cultural polish to enhance their positions in society while distancing themselves from their bootstrap beginnings.

These self-created American aristocrats lived like royalty. Coats of arms were produced, and footmen in livery, ladies' maids, and French chefs served in almost every household. For these few, when the majority of Americans earned an average of $7 a week, it was a time of almost unimaginable luxury, the height of the Gilded Age.

History of the Estate

Hyde Park, Frederick Vanderbilt's newly purchased estate, was first developed during the British colonial period. The area now known as the town of Hyde Park, New York, was granted by the King of England to certain individuals when New York was a colonial province of the Crown. One grantee was Pierre (Peter) Fauconnier, whose portion of the land included the present site of the Vanderbilt mansion. Fauconnier called his estate Hyde Park in honor of his benefactor to whom he was secretary, Edward Hyde, Viscount Cornbury, the provincial Governor of New York.

On his death Fauconnier willed his share of the land grant to his daughter,

Magdalena Valleau, who subsequently sold her share to her son-in-law, Dr. John Bard. During the last half of the eighteenth century, John Bard was a physician of considerable reputation in New York City. His son Samuel was also a physician who trained in Europe, receiving his medical degree with distinction. While living abroad, Samuel Bard developed a lifelong interest in botany and horticulture.

In 1772, John Bard retired from New York City to his Hyde Park estate, known as the Red House, which was located on the east side of the Albany Post Road. Samuel Bard remained in New York City, continuing to practice and teach medicine. Both Bards remained loyal to the British, despite the fact that most of John Bard's neighbors in the Hudson valley were dedicated patriots. The Bards must have adapted to the changes wrought by victory, however, since both served as physician to George Washington during the first years of American independence.

In 1795 Samuel built a large house with a garden at Hyde Park. He chose a natural plateau elevated about 300 feet above the river which commanded a magnificent view of the river valley and the mountains beyond. This house was the first of several to stand on the present site of the Vanderbilt Mansion. Along with the house he built a greenhouse, said to be the first in Dutchess County.

John Bard deeded Hyde Park to his son Samuel in 1797, the year before he died. Samuel continued to live in his house on the estate until his death in 1821 at the age of seventy-nine. His wife, Mary, died the next day. William Bard, their only surviving son, then inherited Hyde Park, which despite the sale of some portions, still constituted 540 acres. William lived there until 1828, when he sold the estate to Dr. David Hosack of New York City.

Hosack had been a student of, and later, a partner in medical practice with Samuel Bard, and had visited often at Hyde Park. Like the Bards he was interested in botany and scientific agriculture. The fortune of Hosack's third wife, Magadalene Coster, allowed him to become a gentleman farmer at Hyde Park.

Hosack spent thousands of dollars on improvements and construction at Hyde Park. He hired André Parmentier, a noted Belgian landscape architect, to plan the park, roads, paths, and gardens of the estate. Parmentier left a remarkable legacy to all succeeding owners of Hyde Park, each of whom retained Parmentier's naturalistic style and enhanced it through their love of horticulture and farming.

David Hosack died on December 22, 1835, at the age of sixty-six. In 1840, the house built by Samuel Bard and 108 surrounding acres were sold to John Jacob Astor for $42,000. Astor made a gift of his purchase to his daughter, Dorothea Langdon, and her five children. Her son Walter Langdon, Jr., eventually bought out the interests of his family and by 1852 became sole owner.

The Bard-Hosack house was destroyed by fire in 1845. In 1847, Walter Langdon reconstructed the mansion on its former site. Then in 1872, Langdon purchased the farmland east of the Post Road, and thereby restored the estate to its original size. However, the Hyde Park mansion was closed for years since the Langdons spent most of their time in Europe. In 1882, Walter Langdon returned to Hyde Park where he lived until his death in 1894.

Construction of The Mansion

When Frederick and Louise Vanderbilt acquired Hyde Park in 1895 from the estate of Walter Langdon, they retained the noted architects, McKim, Mead, and White, of New York to design new wings for the north and south ends of the house. In addition they wanted to renovate and upgrade the existing structure.

McKim, Mead, and White soon discovered that the wooden supporting beams in the old mansion were riddled with dry rot, and that there were structural problems in the foundation. They recommended that the Vanderbilts raze the house and begin again. Thoroughly disheartened by this news, Louise Vanderbilt contemplated building an English-style country house rather than recreate the afflicted building. The architects persuaded her to accept a design modeled after the original mansion, but with interior modifications and a structure that was virtually rotproof and fireproof. The new house had an exterior of Indiana limestone around a brick core and an interior of plaster and marble. The structure was supported by steel I-beams and concrete, making the Vanderbilt Mansion one of the first private residences to use steel beams.

So that they might observe and enjoy the construction of the mansion, the Vanderbilts asked the architects to design a lodge for them to use as temporary housing. Located on the bluff just north of the mansion, the lodge was constructed in sixty-six working days, at a cost of more than $50,000. The Vanderbilts moved in during November, 1895. Later the lodge, which they named the Pavilion, was used as an overflow guest house, primarily for bachelor friends. Frederick and Louise also used the Pavilion as a winter weekend retreat, where they entertained with skating and sleighing parties, maintaining there a year-round staff.

The mansion was built within two years by Norcross Brothers of Boston. Crews worked elbow to elbow, in twelve-hour shifts, stopping only during the coldest months. The men lived in a tent city in front of the mansion. Most of the construction was completed by the winter of 1898, but it took European craftsmen until April, 1899, to sculpt and mold the elaborate marble and plasterwork interior. At completion, the mansion had approximately fifty rooms on four different levels, including servants' quarters, laundry, and cooking facilities. The cost for construction alone was more than $600,000 with construction workers earning an average of $1.50 a day. By the time the mansion was decorated and furnished by the noted designers Ogden Codman and Georges A. Glaenzer, the total cost has been estimated at $2,250,000. The size of the mansion and grounds can best be realized upon learning that there were over 60 full time employees. Of this number, 17 worked in the house, 2 in the pavilion and 44 on the grounds and farm.

Frederick Vanderbilt was intrigued with hydroelectric power after seeing a demonstration at a fair. Frederick built a hydroelectric system with a generating plant at Crum Elbow Creek on the estate grounds, making the mansion one of the first private homes in the Hudson Valley to have electricity.

In addition to underground electrical service, the mansion was furnished with the most modern conveniences of the period. Two coal-fired furnaces supplied central warm air heat for the first and second floors of the building and steam radiation for the basement and third floors. The house had hot and cold running water, indoor plumbing with flush toilets, and silver-plated bathroom fixtures.

While the mansion was being built, Frederick directed considerable activity elsewhere on the estate. Through extensive forestry work, including the moving and replanting of trees, he recreated the park-like beauty of the grounds. He completed water systems, a powerhouse, new greenhouses, a new steel reinforced bridge spanning Crum Elbow Creek at the estate entrance, and a stable-coach house. Later, he supervised the repair of the farm buildings east of Albany Post Road and the installation of new roads on the farm section.

Despite the fact that its fundamental design was based on the house built by Samuel Bard in 1795 and rebuilt by William Langdon in 1847, the Vanderbilt Mansion emerged at its completion in 1899 as an eclectic interpretation of the Italian Renaissance style. McKim, Mead, and White were trained at l'Ecole des Beaux Arts in Paris. They and other American builders prominent at the turn of the century were strongly influenced by the Beaux Arts fascination with both French and Italian Renaissance architecture.

For some years after 1900, Frederick continued to make changes at Hyde Park. He built new barns; he commissioned the landscape architect James L. Greenleaf to plant an extensive terraced formal Italian garden; he acquired additional land; and he completed some final changes on the mansion interior. The estate then took on the appearance that is preserved today.

The Family

Frederick William Vanderbilt was the grandson of Cornelius Vanderbilt (1794-1877), founder of the family fortune, and progenitor of more than 900 descendants alive today. Cornelius' Dutch forebears had settled and farmed on Staten Island, New York, during the seventeenth century.

Cornelius was an enterprising young man who parlayed a $100 loan from his mother into a fortune. He purchased a small boat which he used to ferry goods and people between Manhattan and Staten Island. Because he kept with strict punctuality to scheduled runs, he rapidly acquired a reputation in New York

Harbor that allowed him to expand his business. Having recognized their potential, he soon expanded his business into steamboats, achieving a near monopoly of all harbor and river traffic. Although Cornelius was unschooled and rough-spoken, his native shrewdness and acumen allowed him to best his competition. His shipping business earned him the unofficial title of *Commodore*.

He was later persuaded by his son William Henry to invest in railroads. Converting his capital from shipping, Cornelius began to buy up the railways left dilapidated and impoverished by both mismanagement and economic conditions resulting from the Civil War. By 1867 he had gained control of the New York Central Railroad. When he died in 1877, Cornelius Vanderbilt left the bulk of his $105,000,000 estate to his second eldest son, William Henry. His thirteen other children received small settlements and trust funds.

William Henry Vanderbilt married Maria Louise Kissam, and they became parents of four sons and four daughters. Upon his death in 1885, William divided most of his holdings almost equally between Cornelius II and William Kissam, his first and second sons. Cornelius II became head of the Vanderbilt family. The remainder of the estate, in the form of capital, stocks, and trust funds, he left to his two younger sons, Frederick and George, and his daughters. In the eight years after his father's death, the quiet and steady William had shrewdly doubled his inheritance, but did not live to enjoy the fruits of his labor.

Frederick William Vanderbilt was born on February 2, 1856. He was a quiet child, interested in science and literature. Although he and his brothers all attended school, Frederick was the only one to complete his education. He received a degree in horticulture from the Sheffield Scientific School at Yale University in 1878. Soon after graduation, he married Louise Anthony Torrance and took his place in the family business. He and his three brothers all served the family's railroad interests in one capacity or another in the various offices of the New York Central Railroad in New York City.

Naturally modest and retiring, Frederick quietly invested his inherited fortune of twelve million dollars or so into extremely well-diversified holdings. He sat on the boards of numbers of corporations, including twenty-two rail lines. He took pride in the New York Central's punctual timetables and rarely took advantage of his special status with the railroad, preferring to travel on regular trains rather than use his private rail car.

Frederick was not able to develop his scientific and horticultural interests fully until he and Louise purchased Hyde Park. Throughout most of their marriage the Vanderbilts regulated their lives according to the seasons, as did all the members of their set at the turn of the century. During the winter months and through the New Year, they lived at their New York City townhouse for the social season. From there they traveled to the warmer climes of Florida, California, or the Riviera, where they stayed in rented houses until spring. In early spring, they returned to Hyde Park, usually staying until the Fourth of July. For the rest of the summer they moved to one of their several summer places at

Newport, Bar Harbor, or Upper St. Regis Lake, or perhaps they cruised the Mediterranean. Autumn would bring them back to Hyde Park, where they remained until after Thanksgiving. Then once again they returned to New York City for the season, leaving only to spend Christmas at Hyde Park.

Each of Frederick William's brothers built extravagant and pretentious mansions of the most costly materials. His youngest brother, George, built and continually developed his chateau, Biltmore, in Asheville, North Carolina, which eventually depleted his fortune. His brother Cornelius II built the Breakers, and his brother William Kissam, Marble House, both in Newport, Rhode Island. These architectural wonders stand as monuments to the ostentatious competition which was so prevalent in the Vanderbilts' circle. Frederick's mansion, while built and furnished in the grand manner, is not so flamboyant as his brothers' houses. While the Hyde Park house has been called "a vulgar pile," it has also been described as "homelike," if such an adjective can be applied to a dwelling of fifty rooms. In any case, Frederick seems to have been uninterested in a competition with the rest of the family.

Frederick apparently was more interested in pursuing his two enthusiasms of horticulture and yachting. Yachting was a tradition with Vanderbilt men dating back to the first Cornelius and his ocean-going steam yacht, the *North Star*. Over his lifetime, Frederick, a noted yachtsman, sponsored American entries in a number of international competitions, including the America's Cup Race.

In his later years, Frederick became almost reclusive. He rarely spoke to his staff, preferring to pass along instruction through his housekeeper or superintendent. Yet he was considerate and generous to his staff and indulgent to his wife. He managed his affairs and holdings so well that he not only survived the stock market crash in 1929 and the Great Depression, but prospered through it. His philanthropies were many, but, because he carefully avoided the limelight, his gifts were not generally publicized. Columbia University Medical School, the Salvation Army, and Vanderbilt University all benefited from his largesse.

After Louise died in 1926, Frederick retired to Hyde Park. Here he lived in quiet solitude, seeing only close friends and family. His bereavement caused him to move from the master bedroom suite to a small guest room on the third floor of the mansion. He lived out the remainder of his life at this, his favorite home, enjoying the gardens, grounds, and farm which had drawn him there so many years before.

Frederick William Vanderbilt died on June 29, 1938, at Hyde Park. He was eighty-two years old. Since he and Louise had no children, he bequeathed the estate to Margaret Louise Van Alen (Mrs. James), a niece of Louise. Two years later, Mrs. Van Alen gave Hyde Park to the Federal Government in memory of her Uncle Frederick. On December 18, 1940, Vanderbilt Mansion was designated a National Historic Site, "... as representative and illustrative of its period, is of national significance in the economic, sociological, and cultural history of this country...." The house and grounds are open throughout the year.

The Reception Hall

The Den

The Pool House, Italian Gardens

Roadside splendor

The Steinway concert grand piano, the Living Room

Louis XV clock detail

Louise Vanderbilt's Bedroom

Southwest view, Hudson River

The Lower Gatehouse

The east façade

The Reception Room

The Dining Room

A corner of the Living Room

The South Portico

A Living Room detail

The Mansion from the west bank of the Hudson River

The Kitchen

A Hudson River panorama

The Coach House and Stable

Crum Elbow Creek

The Grand Staircase

The balustrade on the White Bridge

The Blue Room

A painted ceiling panel   37

The Carriage Road

Crum Elbow Creek

The Rose Garden

The Indiana limestone exterior

An electrical wall sconce

Frederick Vanderbilt's Bedroom

Frederick Vanderbilt's Study

The Hudson River from the North Overlook

A wall carving in the Den

The Mansion at dawn

An Italian urn graces the West Portico